P9-CQW-158

CH

1251 97237

Make·a·Saurus

MY LIFE WITH RAPTORS AND OTHER DINOSAURS

by **BRIAN COOLEY** and **MARY ANN WILSON**

ANNICK PRESS

TORONTO + NEW YORK + VANCOUVER

DEDICATION

This book is dedicated to our parents, Lawrence and Dorothy, Barb and Ted, for their unconditional love and support.

ACKNOWLEDGMENTS

We would like to express our gratitude to the paleontologists all over the world who toil in less than ideal conditions to bring us the images of a world long disappeared. In particular, we would like to thank the wonderful people at The Royal Tyrrell Museum of Paelaeontology, Drumheller, Alberta, especially Dr. Philip Currie.

We would also like to thank *National Geographic* magazine for involving us in the excitement surrounding the new discovery of feathered dinosaurs at Laioning.

Cataloguing in Publication Data

Cooley, Brian
    Make-a-saurus : my life with raptors and other dinosaurs

ISBN 1-55037-645-4 (bound) ISBN 1-55037-644-6 (pbk.)

1. Dinosaurs — Models — Juvenile literature. I. Wilson, Mary Ann, 1955 – . II. Title.

QE862.D5C696 2000   j567.9'022'8   C00-930805-9

Editing by Elizabeth McLean
Cover and interior design by Irvin Cheung/iCheung Design
Cover photography by Gary Campbell
The text was typeset in Perpetua and Triplex.

We acknowledge the support of the Canada Council for the Arts, the Ontario Arts Council, and the Government of Canada through the Book Publishing Industry Development Program (BPIDP) for our publishing activities.

Distributed in Canada by	Published in the USA by	Distributed in the USA by
Firefly Books Ltd.	Annick Press (U.S.) Ltd.	Firefly Books (U.S.) Inc.
3680 Victoria Park Avenue		P.O. Box 1338
Willowdale, ON		Ellicott Station
M2H 3K1		Buffalo, NY 14205

Printed and bound in Canada by Kromar Printing Ltd.

Visit our website at www.annickpress.com

Contents

Foreword

IMAGINE BEING ASKED TO CREATE A PREHISTORIC SCENE OF DINOSAURS.

Perhaps a Tyrannosaurus will tangle with a horned dinosaur. Pterosaurs will fly in the skies of your scene. Duck-billed dinosaurs herd near an ancient lakeshore. How would you begin? How would you know what anything looks like? This is the challenge that faces every artist who recreates the past.

The only evidence we have of what creatures from the age of dinosaurs looked like are their fossil remains. But some artists, such as Brian Cooley, are able to combine the information scientists get from fossils with their own knowledge of animal anatomy and behavior — as well as their artistic skills — to create believable creatures. It is their art that we lean on to see back in time. These artists are the ones who put flesh on ancient bones to breathe life into things long dead. Their creations are the result of years of training, research and experience as well

as inspiration and just plain hard work. Without their vision, we would be very blind to the past.

I've been fortunate to work with many artists who make a living bringing the past to life. One of the most rewarding experiences has been working with sculptor Brian Cooley to model several amazing new dinosaurs discovered in China. When news came of these "feathered" dinosaurs, it caused a sensation in the media. Brian Cooley's models created for *National Geographic* magazine were seen by millions of people around the world. It is through his efforts, and the work of many scientists and other artists, that our view of what prehistoric life may have looked like is becoming clearer every day.

Christopher Sloan
ART DIRECTOR
National Geographic magazine

WHEN I WAS SIX YEARS OLD, I FOUND A PLASTIC DINOSAUR IN A BOX OF CEREAL.

What a fateful day that was! That model fired me up so much I went on to collect more plastic dinosaurs, and read everything I could about those remarkable animals. Eventually, it led me into a career of collecting and studying dinosaur fossils. Today, I work in a wonderful facility, The Royal Tyrrell Museum of Palaeontology in Drumheller, Alberta, Canada, in the badlands where dinosaur fossils are abundant.

I have many opportunities to work with creative people who portray dinosaurs in different ways. Among all of the artists, cartoonists, film makers and writers I have worked with over the years, one of my longest and most fruitful associations has been with Brian Cooley and Mary Ann Wilson, the authors of this book.

Brian's artistic ability, knowledge of dinosaur anatomy and attention to detail have made him one of the world's top dinosaur sculptors. He is the ideal person to guide you through the process of creating your own dinosaurs.

Even with all my training and experience, I still learn a lot when Brian asks me how the bones of a skeleton actually go together. Often we end up pulling bones out of the Museum's collections so we can consider how they fit together and how the muscles were attached.

Most people can learn more by building models than by just looking at museum displays and books. If you wish to make your dinosaurs as accurate as possible, there are many resources to help. It's also fun

Brian Cooley, on left, with Dr. Philip Currie

to create dinosaurs from your imagination. You can use your artistic talents to make them esthetically pleasing or to strike terror into the hearts of your friends.

More than anything else, always have fun as you embark on your project!

Philip J. Currie
CURATOR OF DINOSAURS
Royal Tyrrell Museum
of Palaeontology

Introduction

LIKE MOST CHILDREN, I WAS FASCINATED BY DINOSAURS.

I READ EVERY BOOK I COULD FIND ON THE SUBJECT, COLLECTED

SMALL PLASTIC ONES, BUILT MODEL KITS AND

MADE MY OWN DINOSAUR SCULPTURES AND LANDSCAPES.

I DREW HUNDREDS OF PICTURES OF MY FAVORITE DINOSAURS—

NEVER DREAMING HOW MANY DINOSAURS

HAD YET TO BE DISCOVERED.

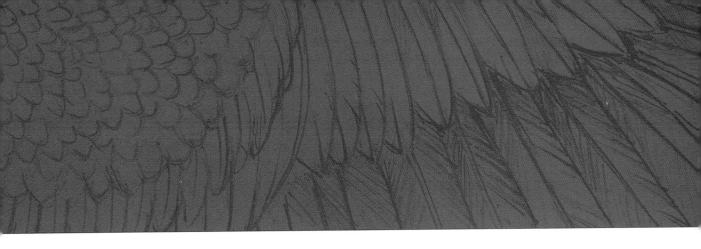

SOMETIMES I WOULD CUT OUT ONE WALL OF A CARDBOARD BOX AND USE THE BOTTOM AND

REMAINING THREE SIDES TO CREATE DIFFERENT ENVIRONMENTS. SO THAT THE DINOSAURS FELT

AT HOME, I MADE SWAMPS, TREES AND ROCKS FOR THEM. I PAINTED BACKGROUNDS ON THE BOX

WALLS. OTHER TIMES, WHEN THE WEATHER WAS NICE, I USED A LARGE PATCH OF EARTH

BEHIND MY HOUSE TO BUILD EVEN BIGGER SWAMPS FILLED

WITH WATER. LOOMING OVER THEM WERE VOLCANOES MADE OF PILED

DIRT. TRANSPLANTED WEEDS COMPLETED MY IMAGINARY WORLD.

ife takes us in marvelous directions and, as luck would have it, the first job I found upon graduating from art school was sculpting a volcano for the Calgary Zoo's new Prehistoric Park. That led to making a dinosaur for a company in Vancouver. My wife, artist Mary Ann Wilson, worked on that dinosaur with me, and since then we have completed many dinosaurs together. While doing research for that project, Mary Ann and I met Dr. Philip J. Currie, who was soon to become one of the world's most prominent paleontologists. It was Dr. Currie whose enthusiasm and riveting stories about new discoveries and theories rekindled my passion for dinosaurs.

Twenty years since that meeting, I'm still making dinosaurs—only now, instead of terrorizing my back yard as they did in my childhood, they go to such places as The Royal Tyrrell Museum of Palaeontology in Drumheller, Alberta, The Academy of Natural Sciences in Philadelphia and The Field Museum of Natural History in Chicago. Sometimes they invade television programs and magazines such as *National Geographic*.

It's still great fun for me to imagine what dinosaurs really looked like and how they lived— and to create that world with my own hands. Although some of the techniques I use are difficult and expensive, anyone with a little imagination and enthusiasm can bring their own prehistoric world to life simply and inexpensively. This book will show you how.

It's still great fun for me to imagine
what dinosaurs really looked like
and how they lived—
and to create that world

Our Changing
View of Dinosaurs

Our image of dinosaurs has changed since I was a small child. Back then, scientists believed that all dinosaurs were cold-blooded reptilian plodders, dragging their tails through a swampy, volcano-infested landscape. Occasionally, individuals would bump into each other and clumsily battle to the death. With their walnut-sized brains, it was assumed that dinosaurs were truly stupid beasts.

However laughable we might find such ideas today, the paleontologists (scientists who study ancient life) and artists of my childhood had described a world full of creatures so compelling that it fired the imagination of millions of children, including me.

with my own hands.

Over the years, our understanding and our image of dinosaurs changed a great deal. They still weren't very smart compared to a lot of modern animals, but now their tails had been lifted into the air and were no longer being dragged through the mud. We started to think of dinosaurs as more graceful. The plant-eating dinosaurs known as herbivores lived in gigantic herds and the meat eaters, called carnivores, sometimes hunted in packs. Discoveries of nests full of eggs and babies suggested that some types of dinosaurs looked after their young.

Scientists pointed out that some of the dinosaurs had skeletons very similar to the skeletons of birds, and today we are certain that some of the dinosaurs were warm-blooded. Warm-blooded animals, such as mammals and birds, make their own body heat, while cold-blooded animals, such as reptiles and amphibians, need to get their heat from warm air or the hot sun. A warm-blooded dinosaur could run faster for a longer time than a cold-blooded one. Suddenly we imagined them as swift, dynamic creatures speeding across the land.

There was one problem with the new idea that dinosaurs were warm-blooded. As you know, birds and mammals, unlike

Sinornithosaurus

The World of
Sinornithosaurus

In Laioning, northeastern China, rolling hills are covered with a thin layer of soil and short grass. The climate is cool and relatively dry. Near the village of Sihetun, there is a place where colored layers of rock lie stacked like the pages of a giant book. The fossil stories they tell describe a much different world.

One hundred and twenty million years ago, the air was warm. Frequent rainfall mixed with the ash snakes and lizards and frogs, almost always have a covering of fur or feathers to keep warm when the air is cool. The exceptions are the really big animals such as elephants, which are able to hold heat in their giant bodies without needing a coat. Many paleontologists feel that the smaller dinosaurs would have needed feathers or fur if they had been warm-blooded. Otherwise, they would have been too cold to survive. There is even the possibility that young offspring of large meat-eaters

Photo by O. Louis Mazzatenta

Fossil of Sinornithosaurus

such as Tyrannosaurus rex had fur or feathers until they grew larger. But it's a rare day when all of the scientists in the world agree about something. Today, some scientists still feel it's pre-

posterous for us to think dinosaurs were warm-blooded. One of the arguments used was that no fossils showing dinosaurs with feathers or fur had ever been found.

of active volcanoes to nourish lush vegetation. Streams and lakes were full of fish, frogs and crocodiles. The air was alive with the buzz of insects. Primitive birds such as Confuciusornis (con-few-see-us-**or**-nis), flew through the sky trailing their long, forked tails. Feathered dinosaurs roamed the forests, some at least 2 metres (6 1/2 feet) long! Snakes, lizards and smaller mammals kept a wary eye out for one of the most feared small predators of its day, Sinornithosaurus. Growing to over a metre (3 feet) long, Sinornithosaurus was a swift, agile hunter with nearly 60 daggerlike teeth and big, terrible claws. Most likely, it was smarter than the other creatures upon which it preyed. It looked and probably behaved much like Velociraptor, a 1.8-metre-long (6 feet) dinosaur that lived many millions of years after

Sinornithosaurus. In fact, Sinornithosaurus is considered a possible ancestor of Velociraptor (vel-**aw**-sih-rap-tore).

No matter how cunning and vicious, all creatures are in constant danger from the forces of nature. The volcanoes far to the west were constantly erupting. Along with ash, they sometimes brought poisonous gas. Creatures were killed by the thousands. Many, such as the Sinornithosaurus skeleton that was recently discovered, fell, or were blown into the lakes where a blanket of fine ash covered them and preserved their remains for 120 million years.

Scientists have just begun to peel back the pages of the giant stone book in Laioning. The stories they tell will thrill us for years. No doubt we will learn much more about Sinornithosaurus and the world it lived in.

In 1971, an expedition of paleontologists from Poland set out to look for dinosaurs in the Gobi Desert of Mongolia. There they uncovered one of the most spectacular finds in the history of paleontology — the fossil of a Velociraptor in the process of killing a Protoceratops (pro-toe-**sair**-a-tops). Velociraptor had grasped its victim by the frill with its forelimbs and, using the huge claw on one of its hind feet, was ripping at the throat of Protoceratops.

It was a bad day for both of them, because Protoceratops locked onto one of Velociraptor's forelimbs with its massive beak and they died together, either in a sandstorm or the collapse of a sand dune. The good thing is that it gave us a clear idea of how Velociraptor and their relatives, such as Sinornithosaurus, killed their prey.

Feather impressions can be clearly seen in this close-up of the Sinornithosaurus fossil.

Photo by O. Louis Mazzatenta

The wonderful thing about paleontology is that new discoveries are always being made. In 1996, amazing 80- to 120-million-year-old fossils were found in China. They showed what were clearly dinosaurs that had been covered with feathers.

We know they were dinosaurs because they had the same kind of skeletons as T. rex and Velociraptor. We know they had feathers because some of the fossils show perfect imprints of feathers growing right out of the front limbs, tail and body.

One of these newly discovered dinosaurs has been named Sinornithosaurus (sigh-nor-nih-tho-**sore**-us), which means "Chinese bird-reptile" (see The World of Sinornithosaurus on pages 4 and 5).

The photographs on pages 4 and 6 also show a sculpture of Sinornithosaurus that I created for *National Geographic* magazine. In order to make the sculpture as realistic as possible, I studied the fossil images carefully. I also consulted with paleontologists Dr. Philip Currie and Dr. Xiao Wu, a scientist from China who has studied Sinornithosaurus extensively.

Bringing
Sinornithosaurus
to Life

In this section, I'll explain how I work and show you how Sinornithosaurus was made from start to finish. After that, I'll show you how to make your own dinosaurs, complete with feathers or a pebbly, lizardlike skin texture.

Getting the Facts First

Sculpture of Protarchaeopteryx

When making any dinosaur, feathered or otherwise, first I need to know what the skeleton looks like and how big the bones are. If I don't, the head won't be the right size compared to the body, the legs and tail won't be the right length, and so on. I always begin a dinosaur sculpture by talking to paleontologists, measuring skeletons and reading whatever has been written about the dinosaur I want to make. I also take lots of photographs of whatever bones are available, so I have something to refer to while I'm working.

Sometimes the fossils I have to work with are a little messy and incomplete. When that happens, I ask the paleontologists what they think the missing parts looked like and whether there are any related dinosaurs that we know more about.

Not long ago, I was asked to create a sculpture of Protarchaeopteryx (pro-tar-kee-**op**-tur-iks) for the Fukui Dinosaur Museum in Japan. Protarchaeopteryx is another recent discovery from China.

It was approximately 80 centimetres (32 inches) long and 60 centimetres (24 inches) high. Its fossil revealed arms, legs and a backbone that were all quite clear and easy to measure. But the head was just a blur with a few teeth sticking out of it. After scratching my own head for a while, trying to imagine the whole animal, I asked Dr. Philip Currie of The Royal Tyrrell Museum of Palaeontology what he thought. He knew for sure that it had enormous front teeth. He also knew from careful study of the skeleton that it shared many characteristics with the flying pigeon-sized dinosaur, Archaeopteryx (ar-kee-**op**-tur-iks), as well as the raptors, such as Dromaeosaurus (**droe**-mee-oh-sore-us) and Velociraptor. He suggested that I make the head look like something halfway between those dinosaurs, so that is what I did.

I got lucky with Sinornithosaurus. The skeleton was nearly complete and beautifully preserved. This dinosaur was also very closely related to Dromaeosaurus and Velociraptor. That made it easy to guess what the only missing part – the end of the tail – looked like.

I usually take skeletal measurements and photographs of skeletons, but in this case the Sinornithosaurus fossil was in China, so rather than fly there I had measurements and photos sent to me. After consultation with Dr. Currie and Dr. Wu, I made some sketches of how I thought the dinosaur would look and what pose I thought it should be in.

I create rough sketches and detailed drawings of possible poses.

Making the Initial Sculpture

Once I am happy with the pose, it is time to begin the armature. An armature is a stiff, sticklike frame that will support the sculpture, much the way your own skeleton supports the rest of your body. I like to use pieces of rigid steel rod welded together. This requires a welder, a tool that melts the steel so I can join the pieces. First I cut steel rods to the exact size as the bones they represent. Using pliers to position them, I weld the rods in the pose that I like.

The next step is to make claws out of epoxy putty (a pasty resin), which becomes hard when it sets. I apply the putty to the steel armature and give the claws a rough shape while they're soft, then file and sand them when they are hard. In the same way, I create a skull, jaws and a set of teeth to be added later. As well as being more realistic, there is another good reason for making hard claws and teeth. When I'm

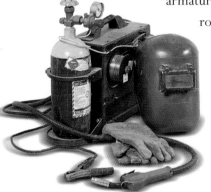

Mini-mig welder, helmet and gloves

The armature is shown here with its carefully sculpted skull and claws over a steel skeleton.

Paleontologists are the world's time travel experts. They find, study and describe the remains of animals that have been gone from this earth for millions and millions of years. It's not always easy for them to explain their findings in a way that the average person can understand. Artists such as me are like interpreters who translate the paleontologists' years of work and research into drawings, paintings and sculptures that everyone can see.

While the artist is always indebted to the scientists who constantly present new information, our work is often of value to them. By turning their knowledge into works of art, we provide a way for them to stand back and look at an idea. We've also provided, over the years, a visual record of how people's way of thinking about dinosaurs has changed.

To be sure I don't run out, I keep almost two tonnes of clay in my workshop.

sculpting, I always bump them. If they're soft, they get all mushed out of shape and I have to keep fixing them. There is one problem, though. The claws and teeth are sharp, which means I sometimes scratch myself!

When the claws are done, I begin adding modeling clay to the armature. Many different kinds of clay are available. Water-based clays are easy to work with, but you need to keep spraying your sculpture with water or it will dry out and crack. Oil-based clays, such as Plasticine and wax clay, don't dry out for years. When I make a big dinosaur, I use Klean Klay, which is soft, oil-based and

non-toxic. To be sure I don't run out, I keep almost two tonnes of it in my workshop! For small dinosaurs such as Sinornithosaurus, I use a harder, oil-based wax clay so that details such as toes will hold their shape.

No matter which clay I choose, I have many tools to help form the clay. Large tools let me fill in large areas quickly, then I use smaller tools as the sculpture becomes more detailed. I shape the clay as though it were muscles attached to the metal bones of my armature. After studying a lot of animal anatomy, I can make educated guesses about where muscles would have attached to bones and how big they were.

At first, the sculpture looks rough. I always work on the whole dinosaur at once, with equal attention to each part. One of the worst mistakes I can

make is to work on one area for a long time without paying attention to the rest of the sculpture. I can end up with details that are in the wrong spot and a sculpture that looks awkward or

Back in the 1800s, an artist named Waterhouse Hawkins created the world's first sculpture of a dinosaur called Iguanodon (ih-**gwon**-o-don). He and his scientific colleagues, working with very little information, produced a piece of art only vaguely resembling Iguanodon, and today we look upon his work with a certain amount of amusement. Yet there is also a great deal of respect, because it was the first attempt to pull an animal from an unimaginably distant past and bring it into the present.

And so it has been ever since: artists working with paleontologists, trying to figure out how the dinosaurs and other prehistoric creatures really looked. We'll never know for sure, but we keep getting closer.

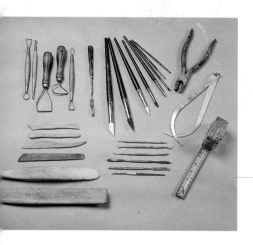

Basic sculpting tools.

Adding the first lump of clay to the armature.

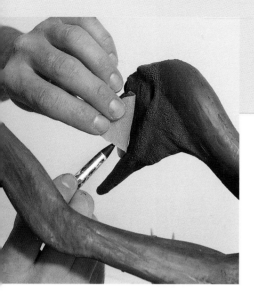

**Texturing the head
with a rubber pad.**

lopsided. If I am unhappy with something, it's easy to make changes at this point.

When the overall form is the way I want it, I do the final shaping. During this stage, muscles become clearly defined, details such as eyelids and toes are finished, and everything is carefully smoothed with clay shaping tools.

Now I start creating the skin texture. For a feathered dinosaur such as Sinornithosaurus, I don't texture the areas that will be covered with feathers. The large scales, such as those on the feet, are made one at a time using a variety of sculpture tools.

Smaller scales are created by pressing textured rubber pads over the surface of the dinosaur. This is very precise work. If I don't press hard enough, the pads don't make a clean impression. If I press too hard, I ruin the shape of the dinosaur. I get the best impression by rolling a tool or even the eraser end of a pencil over the back of the pad.

When I made Sinornithosaurus, I wasn't quite happy with the texturing the first time because the clay was too hard. To fix it, I spread a thin layer of softer, oil-based clay on the areas that needed texture. In the photos, those areas show up as a lighter, fleshy color against the darker brown of the original clay body.

**Sinornithosaurus is
fully sculpted and
ready for skin texture.**

Making the Molds

At last the sculpture looks the way I want. Because the clay is soft, it can easily be damaged simply by touching it. Somehow, it needs to be turned into a hard material. As well, I often need more than one copy of a particular dinosaur. This is where mold-making comes in. A mold is a special container made to reproduce the shape and surface texture of an object. Any plastic toys that you have ever played with came from molds.

To make a mold, the sculpture has to be divided into parts so that when the mold pieces are made, they can be removed from the sculpture. For the mold of Sinornithosaurus, I also cut off both front limbs, one leg and the tail before starting. This may seem awful and scary,

Spraying mold release. You are looking down on the clay wall that divides the sculpture in two. The upright wall running around the dividing wall will contain the liquid rubber.

but it allowed me to make several simple molds instead of a single tricky one. When cutting the sculpture apart, I use a jeweler's saw with a very thin blade to minimize damage. I also get someone else to help hold the dinosaur so that none of the parts fall to the floor after they're cut off.

Each piece is divided in half by building a clay wall, called a parting wall, along the midline. It's best if these walls are a different color than the sculpture. The wall has to be pressed very carefully around the sculpture. If there is any space between the sculpture and the wall, the mold halves won't separate properly. When the walls are in place, round dents called registration keys are pressed into them. They keep the finished mold from shifting. Perhaps you have seen toys where the parts aren't joined properly and there is a ledge at the seam. This happens when the registration keys don't fit correctly.

After the parting walls are finished, the whole sculpture is sprayed with a special substance called mold release. This helps to keep the sculpture from sticking to the mold. I usually use liquid rubber for the mold, because it takes a perfect impression of all the details and it is flexible after it sets. If I used a material that wasn't flexible, I'd never get it to let go of the textured parts of the final sculpture. To make the mold, I pour or brush the rubber mixture onto the sculpture and parting walls. When the

rubber has hardened, I add more layers of rubber until the entire mold is the thickness I want, usually about 5 or 6 millimetres (1/4 inch).

Even though I thicken the rubber with a chemical thickening agent, the mold is still somewhat floppy. Used by itself, a rubber mold would result in a distorted or melted-looking dinosaur – not the effect I want! So I make a stiff jacket or "back-up mold" for the rubber part, out of plaster or fiberglass. Fiberglass is made when polyester resin (a syrupy liquid that becomes a hard plastic when mixed with certain chemicals) is painted into fiberglass matt (glass fibers that have been pressed into a thin sheet and

sealed together with a special glue). I used fiberglass for the Sinornithosaurus. This stuff not only smells bad but is bad for you. Both the fumes and the tiny glass particles are hard on your lungs. It also feels nasty and prickly on your skin. When I work with fiberglass, I wear a respirator mask over my nose and mouth, and rubber gloves on my hands. My studio is also equipped with a powerful fan to suck away the fumes. Before I apply the fiberglass, the rubber has to be completely set and sprayed with a release agent so the jacket doesn't stick to it.

Safely decked out in my protective gear, I mix a paste form of polyester resin that I brush into the uneven areas. This helps

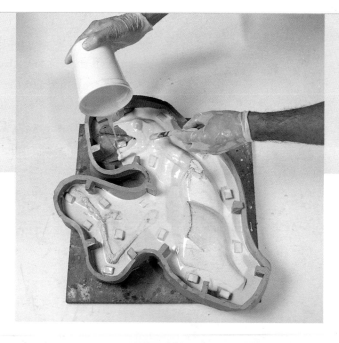

Brushing the first coat of rubber into the skin texture helps eliminate air bubbles.

to prevent air bubbles. Following the paste, I add three layers of fiberglass. When the resin sets, I have a very tough, rigid blanket that holds the rubber in the precise shape needed to make copies of one side of the original sculpture.

So far, I have completed a mold of half a dinosaur. I now have to flip the whole thing over and do the same with the other half. First I remove the clay wall that goes all around the dinosaur. This is when I'm glad to have a wall that is a different color from the sculpture. Once, using the same color for both dinosaur

A rubber mold would result in
a melted-looking dinosaur.

and wall, I gouged part of an Albertosaurus's front limb because I couldn't see the border between it and the dividing wall. I also have to work slowly and carefully to avoid damage. Once the clay wall is removed, I'm looking at a wall of rubber and fiberglass. The second half of my mold is laid up against that. I spray it with mold release, because if I don't, the two sides will stick together and never come apart.

When the second jacket is finished and hardened, the two halves can be pried apart. Again, I have to be careful not to dam-

age the mold or my knuckles. Using screwdrivers or pry bars, I loosen the mold pieces a little at a time, all the way around. If I tried to pry a mold open by simply jamming a tool into a single spot and grunting away, I'd end up with a broken mold and probably some nasty cuts!

When it is finally apart, I usually find part of the sculpture in one half of the mold and the rest in the other. No worries. If the mold has been made properly, I no longer have any use for the original sculpture. I'm ready to make a copy, called a cast, of the dinosaur.

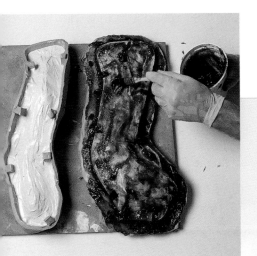

(left) Polyester resin thickened with powders and fibers is brushed onto the set rubber mold of the forelimbs.

(left) The resin is followed by two or three layers of resin-soaked fiberglass matt.

(right) Fiberglass matt makes
the sculpture very strong.

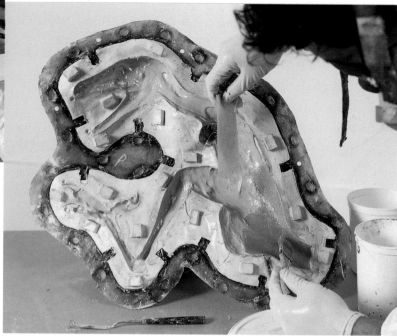

(left) Resin paste fills in all the tiny details.

Casting

Now for the big payoff. The final sculpture needs to be tough and long-lasting. Stinky as it is, I have yet to find anything that works better than fiberglass, so I put on my filter mask and rubber gloves again.

After I remove the original sculpture and any clay bits from the mold, I spray the inside of both halves with mold release. Then I brush in a layer of polyester resin paste. Before the paste hardens, I start laying in strips of fiberglass matt soaked with polyester resin. This is known as the "fiberglass lay-up method." The inside of the cast will be hollow.

For a small dinosaur such as Sinornithosaurus, two layers will probably make it strong enough. I add a third layer just to be safe. You never know when someone is going to drive into it with a forklift.

Once both mold halves have been done, I let the fiberglass set and become hard. I make sure that nothing is sticking up around the edges that will prevent the two halves from fitting together perfectly. Now I want to join the two halves. To ensure that they bond together perma-nently, I spread a bead of resin paste all around both edges, like a noodle of toothpaste squirted out of the tube. I have to work quickly to join the cast pieces before the resin hardens. After I clamp the mold together tightly, I leave it to set overnight. I've learned not to be impatient. It's natural to want to see how well things turned out, but if I open the mold too soon, all my efforts will have been wasted and I'll have to start over.

A perfect casting.

When I make really big dinosaurs, I use three to four layers of fiberglass. Most people don't understand how incredibly strong that much fiberglass is. Once I made a Tyrannosaurus rex for Hitachi Dinoventure in Tokyo, Japan. They were worried that it wouldn't survive an earthquake. I told them that if there was an earthquake powerful enough to damage the T. rex, the dinosaur's well-being would be the least of their concerns. I also expect the six dinosaurs I made for Disney World in Florida to survive any hurricane.

What is chasing?
It certainly doesn't mean running around after the dinosaur.

Assembly

The next day, after a good breakfast and thorough toothbrushing (if my hair is sticking out in all directions it doesn't matter), I pry the mold apart and see how the sculpture looks. The photograph above shows a perfect cast without any air bubbles or missed areas. Now all I have to do is gently remove it from the mold. With the front limbs, leg and tail cast in the same manner, I have a complete dinosaur that is ready for chasing and assembly.

What is chasing, you ask? It certainly doesn't mean running around after the dinosaur. Especially when most of its limbs haven't been attached yet. If you look carefully at even a simple toy such as a Ping Pong ball, you will see little ridges. These mark the place where the pieces were joined to make the whole object. When I remove a sculpture from a mold, the seams are usually a lot more pronounced than the seam on a Ping Pong ball. I want to make them invisible. Making seams invisible and fixing any other flaws is called chasing. Don't ask me why. What I can tell you is that the more careful a person is when mold-making and casting, the less chasing there is. But no matter how careful I have been, I still have to grind the seams away.

In areas where the skin is textured, I end up with a smooth line where I don't want it. To make that line disappear, I spread epoxy putty on the seam, then press a texture pad onto it while it's still soft, as shown on page 18. If it's done right, no one can ever tell where I made the repair.

For unfeathered dinosaurs, I join all the cast pieces with resin paste before I do the chasing. For feathered dinosaurs, however, it's

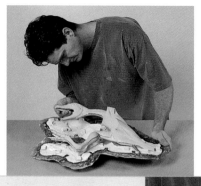

(left) Gently prying
the cast from the mold.

(below) Applying epoxy
putty to the seam.

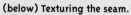

(below) Texturing the seam.

easier to put feathers on the forelimbs and body if they are separate.
I want to be able to join them to the body from time to time to see
how everything looks, though, so I drill holes in the shoulder and the
limb and connect them with a large steel pin. When the forelimbs are
completely finished and the body is feathered all the way up to them,
I glue the pieces together permanently.

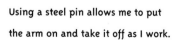

Using a steel pin allows me to put
the arm on and take it off as I work.

Finishing

N ow the hard work is over and I can have some fun. First, I want to give my dinosaur eyes. I drill a hole through the roof of its mouth and grind out a round space behind the eyelids. Then I carefully stick the eyes up through the hole in its mouth and glue them.

Installing the eye is a bit tricky.

You might be wondering where these eyes came from. Sometimes I make my own using colored resins. For really big dinosaurs, I get a glassblower friend to make them for me. Sometimes I can buy glass or plastic eyes from a taxidermy supply store. Taxidermists are people who stuff dead animals and try to make them look as if they're alive. You've probably seen taxidermy animals in museums or other places. Their glass eyes come in handy. Because the head and eye sockets of Sinornithosaurus are the same size as an eagle's, I just bought some eagle eyes from the store.

Taxidermy suppliers sell lots of false animal teeth too. Wolf teeth, bear teeth, fish teeth, you name it. They never have any dinosaur teeth, though. I have to make my own dinosaur dentures. They are like some people's false teeth, only pointier. After the eyes are in place, I fill the hole in the roof of the mouth and glue in the set of teeth, which I made earlier. Then I glue in the tongue, made of epoxy putty on a wire armature.

(above) I paint the claws and feet before I attach the feathers.

(left) I make my own dinosaur dentures.

The last step for unfeathered dinosaurs is painting. Fossils don't tell us anything about what color prehistoric animals were, so we have to guess. I study the colors of modern reptiles and birds, then I decide what I want my sculpture to look like. I also paint the head, feet and hands of feathered dinosaurs before I start attaching the feathers. If I try to paint them after the feathers are on, it will just look messy. Sometimes I paint a pattern on the body to help decide on a color arrangement for the feathers.

Finding the right feathers to cover a dinosaur can be a challenge. We know it's pointless to look for dinosaur feathers, so we have to settle for bird feathers. Scientists are still arguing about whether birds are dinosaurs or whether some dinosaurs were birds, or whether they were even related. The paleontologists I respect most all feel that the strongest evidence favors the theory that dinosaurs were the ancestors of modern birds. I think bird feathers are a lot like dinosaur feathers, so I'm happy to use them. Some hobby stores and sport fishing shops sell many kinds of feathers. Bird farms are another source of feathers.

You'd be surprised how many feathers it takes to cover even a

We know little about the nature of dinosaur feathers at this time. Although Archaeopteryx would have been a poor flyer, fossils clearly show that it had asymmetrical feathers on its wings. This means that the leading edges of the wing feathers were narrow and the trailing edges were wider. All birds that fly have such wing feathers. So far, no asymmetrical feathers have appeared in other dinosaur fossils. This is one reason we don't think of them as flyers.

(above left) Asymmetrical feather
(above right) Symmetrical feather

small dinosaur. I set them all out like paints so I can choose different kinds to make patterns. There are many things to consider before I start to add the feathers. If the belly is lighter than the back, where does the change take place? If there is a pattern, such as stripes, how do the feathers need to be arranged? I usually want small feathers in some places and larger feathers in others, like birds have. The work goes much faster if I make decisions ahead of time and lay the feathers out in order. Of course, one thing

I'm painting a pattern that I will follow when I attach the feathers.

Feathers are sorted according to size, shape, color and pattern.

I've discovered is that the slightest breeze will send the feathers flying all over the room. I've learned not to sigh heavily or let Jack the dog come in wagging his big fluffy tail. One trick that helps the feathers to stay put is to lay them out on sheets of coarse sandpaper. The sandpaper helps to hold the feathers until I'm ready to use them. Still, I have to move carefully. Walking by quickly or even waving my hands around can cause a feather storm.

When gluing the feathers on, I always start from the tail and work forwards, and from the bottoms of the legs upwards. Each feather overlaps the one behind it, so that none of the "skin" shows through. As I said earlier, it's easier to leave the wings detached from the body until all the feathers are on to the point where they join.

Walking quickly or even waving my hands around can cause a feather storm.

Each feather must overlap the one behind it.

The front limbs of Sinornithosaurus aren't actually wings that would have allowed it to fly. It's uncertain exactly what the feathers on its front limbs looked like, so I had to guess at their appearance. This is one of those times when I talk to Dr. Currie and other paleontologists. Because Sinornithosaurus didn't fly, there is no reason to think its front limbs would have closely resembled the wings of modern birds. To come up with a look I liked, I first drew the wing of a modern bird, as shown in the top photo on page 24. Then I drew the front limb of Sinornithosaurus and drew feathers on it until the appearance seemed right to me. Using the drawing as a guide, I trimmed and arranged the feathers to fit it. Before gluing them on to the

The drawing at left shows the wing of a modern flying bird. At right is a possible feather arrangement for Sinornithosaurus.

dinosaur, I stuck a narrow band of tape to the backs of the front limbs to attach the first row. That made it easier to layer the rest of the feathers on top.

The feathers around the face are the very last ones to be attached. I have to be careful to use only a tiny amount of glue. Too much glue will be visible when it's dry and will spoil the natural look of the dinosaur. Once these feathers have been applied, I check the whole sculpture thoroughly for any loose or crooked feathers because it's impossible not to brush against parts of the sculpture when I'm working on other parts. Some feathers always need to be gently coaxed back into place—a bit like brushing your hair in the morning.

Some minor painting touch-ups may also be required if I've missed a spot or accidentally scratched the paint. Then the work is done and the dinosaur is ready for display.

A drawing helps me to determine feather length.

II

Make
Your Own Dinosaur

Now that you've seen how I make a dinosaur, you probably want to get started on your own sculpture right away. I expect you have some terrific ideas you want to try. But first I'll show you some easier and more direct ways to go about it. As you become more experienced, you can consider making molds and trying some of the more complicated steps I use.

Patience is probably the most important skill to learn. Getting the results you want from any art form is strictly a matter of practice. It's quite common for children and adults to be disappointed when they first try to make a sculpture. Trust me. Follow the steps in this book and make a few dinosaurs. You'll create some wonderful results, and ideas for

new ones will come pouring into your mind. You will amaze yourself.

When you're starting out, you don't need all the equipment and expensive materials that I use. Because some of them are potentially hazardous to your health and hard to work with, you're better off beginning without them anyway. The armature is a good example. As much as I

like to begin with a welded steel armature, there are other approaches that work. Welders involve electricity and a lot of heat. They are designed to be used by adults and, as Jordan has just learned in the photograph on the right, even this mini-mig welder is more than mere child's play. You can make a sturdy armature for your dinosaur using the following tools and materials.

Shown below, clockwise from bottom, are some of the tools and materials you may need: scissors; a roll of quick-setting plaster bandages; several kinds of wire, including electrical wire with a plastic coating; mattress foam; flour, water and white glue, for making papier mâché; masking tape; black electrician's tape; newspaper strips, for papier mâché; and dryer lint, for creating details.

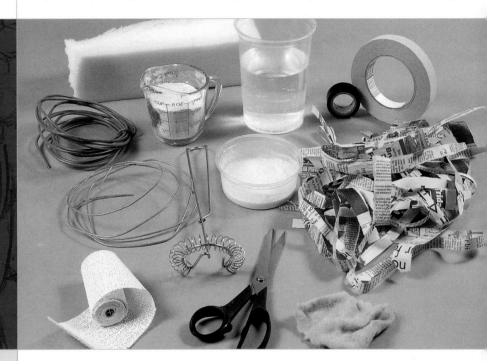

The small gray wad of stuff at the front of the photograph on the right is dryer lint. Dryer lint?! Yes—mixed with glue or other binders, dryer lint is great for creating small details. You can make almost anything with it. It's free and you'd be surprised how much you can collect in a short time. Just volunteer to help with the laundry.

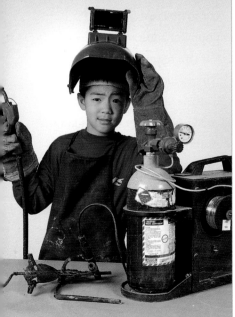

Tools and Materials

The photograph above shows common tools and materials that can be used in a variety of ways. Your parents probably own the tools you'll need. Don't forget to ask before you use tools, though, and be sure to put them back when you finish so they can be found for the next job. The materials are all inexpensive and easy to find. You won't need everything that's listed on the next page, depending on what sort of dinosaur you decide to make.

You won't need this equipment to make your armature.

Hey! Do yourself a favor and read all the instructions in this section before you begin making your dinosaur. I know you're anxious to get started, but you'll be much happier with the results if you have all the information first. Plan to create your dinosaur over several evenings or a weekend, because it takes time for the materials to dry.

TOOLS

- paper
- pencil
- pliers
- wire cutters (or pliers with cutting jaws)
- tweezers
- scissors

MATERIALS

For a wire armature with foam wrapping

- wire *(any wire stiff enough to hold a shape)*
- electrician's tape
- mattress foam
- backer rod (optional)
- masking tape

For a newspaper armature

- newspaper
- masking tape

For covering the armature (3 methods)

- quick-setting plaster bandages
- plaster and burlap fabric
- newspaper, flour and sugar, or white glue
- dryer lint *(to form details such as muscles and eyelids)*

For finishing the sculpture

- stiff wire and electrician's tape *(to make a stand)*
- water-based paints and brushes
- artificial eyes
- comb *(to make teeth)*
- poppy or mustard seeds *(for skin texture)*
- white glue
- feathers or artificial flower petals
- coarse sandpaper *(to hold feathers)*
- water-based, non-toxic contact cement

If we didn't have **skeletons**, we'd look a lot like **water balloons** rolling around on the floor.

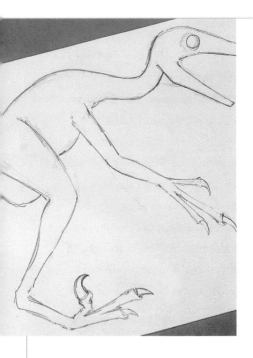

The Sketch

First, of course, you have to decide on the kind of dinosaur you want. There are lots of excellent books available to give your imagination a boost.

Once you have an idea in mind, make a line drawing of the dinosaur, the same size you want your sculpture to be. Tails are generally long and run off the page. Because they are usually simple, it's not necessary to waste a whole sheet of paper on the tail. Don't complicate things by adding detail. This is just a working drawing, not a work of art. It's easiest to only draw one side, as though the other side were invisible. In the drawing shown, the left hind leg and front arms are not sketched in.

The Armature

The next step is to build an armature. The armature is a frame that will support the rest of your sculpture. It acts a little like a skeleton. If we didn't have skeletons, we'd look a lot like water balloons rolling around on the floor. Standing, as we know it, would not be possible and climbing trees would be out of the question. In the same way, an armature keeps your sculpture in the position you want.

Many different materials and methods can be used to make an armature. The ones I will describe are by no means the only possibilities. After following the suggestions in this book, you can probably invent at least one new way by yourself. Rolled-up newspaper, wire, foam and tape, even balloons (if you want a dinosaur that is fat or sausagelike) can all supply the support needed to make your dinosaur stand, run or lay eggs.

In the next pages, I'll show you how to make two kinds of armatures. The first is made by cutting wires and taping them together, then filling out the armature with foam. The second armature is made simply by taping together balls and rolls of newspaper.

Depending on the hardness and thickness of the wire, you may need an older person to help you cut the wire. You have to make sure they don't take over your project, though. Sometimes people start enjoying themselves so much they don't know when to stop helping.

Wire Armature with Foam Wrapping

Using wire cutters or pliers that have cutting jaws, cut and then bend the wire so that it follows the shape of your drawing. Lay the wire on top of your drawing to be sure you have the right shape. The head, neck, body and tail are formed by a single piece of wire. The wire pictured below is electrical wire with a plastic coating, and the separate pieces have been joined with tightly wrapped electrician's tape.

When you are cutting the wire, always cut the pieces longer than you want them. For example, the wires for the toes should be 25 to 30 millimetres (an inch or so) longer. Why? Because the extra length gives you a place to tape the toes to the end of the foot. The same is true for the legs. You'll need the extra length to tape them to the body.

To make two hind legs and two arms, just make the same limb twice, except in mirror image. You don't want a dinosaur with two right hind legs, other-wise it will walk around in circles! Likewise, two left arms will make wrestling difficult.

After you have tightly wrapped the wires together with tape, you can bend the legs into the position you want. If the taping is sloppy and loose, the armature will be too wobbly. In fact, it will probably fall apart before it can become a dinosaur.

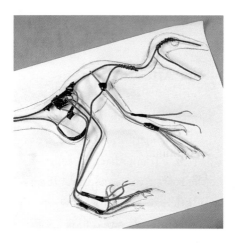

Your sketch is a simple guide for the shape of the armature.

You don't want your dinosaur to have two right legs, or it will walk in circles.

Once your wire armature is to your liking, you can begin to build the dinosaur to its final shape. The photograph below shows a sculpture in progress, so you can see what the different stages look like. I used a different kind of wire for this one, but it does exactly the same job.

Over the wire, I've added mattress foam and held it in place with masking tape. I used mattress foam for the body, legs, tail and head. You can ask for scraps at your local foam mattress shop. Most shops will be glad to sell them for a small cost, or may even give you enough to make your dinosaur. I could have used the same material for the front limbs and neck but, just because I like to try new things, I used something called backer rod. Backer rod is a building material designed to be jammed into the cracks in houses where cold air sneaks in. It's like a thin foam noodle and comes in different sizes. You should be able to find it at one of those big home improvement stores. A lot of smaller hardware stores also carry backer rod. You can do all kinds of nifty things with it.

Despite the wire armature inside, this foam and tape dinosaur is a bit wobbly and it would be nice to stiffen it up. There are a couple of ways to do this. The dinosaur in the photograph on page 32 was made with quick-setting plaster bandages. This is probably the easiest and least messy way, but you can also use plaster and burlap, or papier mâché. These methods are shown on pages 35 to 42.

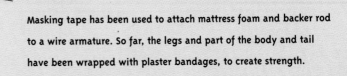

Masking tape has been used to attach mattress foam and backer rod to a wire armature. So far, the legs and part of the body and tail have been wrapped with plaster bandages, to create strength.

(below) Jordan is bending and cutting wire to match the outline of his drawing.

Here, Jordan is taping together one of the feet.

(below) When all of the armature pieces are taped together, Jordan gives it form and strength with plaster.

Jordan is going to make a dinosaur of his own invention—a perfectly acceptable thing to do—and has chosen the wire armature method. He has a sketch and, having wisely abandoned the welder, is all set with pliers and wire in hand.

He begins by cutting and bending the wire to fit the shape of his dinosaur drawing, leaving extra length for joining the pieces. Next he cuts the individual toes and tapes them to the limbs.

Jordan has learned quickly how to tape the wires tightly and in no time has attached all the limbs to the body. The result is a sturdy armature ready to be filled out.

Jordan has decided to add bulk to his dinosaur using mattress foam and masking tape. One person can do this by himself, but it can be hard to hold onto the wire and foam with one hand while you wrap tape around them with the other hand. Don't be afraid to ask for help, even if it's just to hold part of the dinosaur.

After the body is the right shape, Jordan covers the foam with quick-setting plaster bandages. Within an hour, the sculpture is set, and Jordan is ready to finish his dinosaur with eyes, teeth and paint.

Newspaper Armature

Another easy way to start your dinosaur sculpture is by using newspaper to make the armature. If you choose this method, you will need enough newspaper to make a number of balls and tight cylinders. These balls and cylinders will be different sizes, depending on what they will be used for.

The body can be made by squeezing a large ball of newspaper into the shape you want and wrapping it with masking tape to hold its form. You will need to squish the ball tightly in your hands and maybe even pound on it with your fist to get the shape you want. For the head, you can make a smaller ball or perhaps two separate, irregular shapes for the head and lower jaw.

The hind and front limbs will be made of newspaper rolled into cylinders of the right size and length. Toes and fingers are made of much smaller rolls. These cylinders need to be very tightly rolled. Loosely rolling up a little scrap of paper won't do the trick. It may take you a few tries to get the feel of it. You stop the cylinders from unraveling by wrapping them with masking tape. Two things help to make the taping easier. One is simply to ask someone else to tape

while you hold. If there is no one around, precut a number of strips of tape and stick one end to the edge of your work surface.

The photograph above is of two sculptures at different stages. The one in the foreground shows all the parts that make up the dinosaur. Can you tell which parts are scrunched-up balls and which ones are rolled-up cylinders? Standing behind it is a dinosaur after all of the pieces have been taped together, then covered with two or three layers of papier mâché (described on pages 40 to 42).

Miranda's dinosaur as it progresses from balls and cylinders to a dinosaur ready for its papier mâché coat.

In the top left photograph, Miranda has made the major body parts and laid them out so that she has a good idea what her dinosaur is going to look like. The top right photograph shows it taped together, but still missing the feet. In the bottom left photograph, Miranda has just taped three toes together to make a

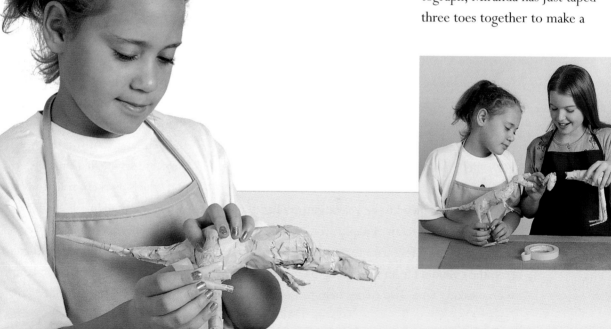

Working with friends is fun, and extra hands help jobs get done quickly.

foot, which she is ready to tape onto the bottom of the leg.

With her dinosaur all taped together, she can take time to help Emily attach the head to her dinosaur. Working with friends is a good idea for several reasons. It's fun, some jobs can be done more quickly with extra hands, and there is a better chance of coming up with new ideas. I've been making dinosaurs professionally for twenty years and I've never made one entirely by myself. A lot of the time I work with my wife, Mary Ann. Other times, I've had as many as five artist friends helping. It's like having six heads and twelve arms! Just remember never to get crusty if you can't agree about something. That's the time to take a break, and do something else for a while.

Giving the Armature Form and Strength

To make your dinosaur strong as well as good-looking, it needs to be covered in a hard material. I'll show you three ways to do this: plaster bandages, plaster and burlap, and papier mâché.

Using plaster bandages is the simplest and fastest method; however, it's also the most expensive. Plaster and burlap are cheaper, but you have to buy them from different sources — usually at opposite ends of town — and you often have to buy more than you need. Although not quite as strong as plaster, papier mâché is very inexpensive and made from materials found in nearly every home.

You can use any of these methods for either type of armature. All are messy, but if you put newspaper under your work area you'll save yourself a lot of work afterward. Soap and water will clean up your hands, and anything you missed covering with newspaper.

Quick-Setting Plaster Bandages

Plaster bandages are generally used by doctors to make stiff casts on broken arms and legs. Perhaps you've owned a cast of your own after some careless and dangerous activity. I have myself on more occasions than I care to admit. To make a cast, the whole roll of bandage is dipped in water and furiously wrapped around the injured limb. Several rolls are used to make one cast.

Just as the plaster bandage holds an arm or leg still until it heals, it will make your dinosaur solid forever. But if you try using whole rolls at a time, you'll run into trouble. Doctors are never trying to make your broken arm or leg look like a dinosaur, so they can work really fast without worrying about the final appearance. You, however, will want to be more thoughtful, and that takes time.

For a cat-sized dinosaur, you'll need about two rolls of bandages. To keep them from becoming as hard as rock before you've put them where you want, cut them into smaller strips. The strips need to be long enough to wrap around your dinosaur at least once. Otherwise, they tend to fall off or hang in unsightly shreds.

Before you begin to wrap, spread newspaper over your work area and set a bowl of water near you. Wet the strips one at a time, then start to wrap your sculpture. Each time you start a new strip, overlap the one you just wrapped. Work on the whole dinosaur as you go. It's easy to end up with one extra-fat leg or another problem if you

Your dinosaur may have a body part that you feel is too small, or you may want to add a feature of some sort, such as a shoulder or a hip. Just wad a wet bandage into a lump, shape it where you want and hold it in place with another bandage wrapped around the dinosaur.

Even the delicate work of wrapping toes is messy.

wrap one part without paying attention to the others.

In the photograph on page 31, you can see that the legs, hips, part of the body and part of the tail have been wrapped in plaster bandages. It's best to do those areas first and let them set,

so that your dinosaur is strong enough to stand. Then work your way out from the center of the dinosaur. The weight of the wet plaster can cause the tail or neck to droop, so you may want to put a box or other support under the end of the tail and under the head.

In the photograph at left you can see that the fingers and toes are each wrapped separately with tiny strips of bandage. Once you've covered your whole dinosaur, let it set until it is dry to the touch. This should take about half an hour—just enough time to clean up even if you forgot to put newspaper under-

neath. I warned you, this is a messy business.

Once the plaster is set, poke the dinosaur all over with your fingers. If any areas still feel soft, give them another layer of bandage. Before adding new plaster over the old bandages, always wet the area first.

Once it's thoroughly hard, you can finish your dinosaur almost any way you want. See pages 43 to 48 for some ideas to get you started.

Doctors are never trying to make your broken arm look like a dinosaur.

Plaster and Burlap

This method is even messier than using plaster bandages and takes a little longer, but it's not as expensive. It works well for larger projects.

When people say plaster, they usually mean plaster of Paris, but there are many other kinds that I use, including potter's plaster—which is faster-setting and harder. Plaster of Paris can be bought at craft and hobby shops, while potter's plaster is found at pottery supply stores and some building supply stores. Burlap is most easily found in large fabric stores.

Before you begin, spread newspaper over your work area to catch drips. Use scissors to cut the burlap into strips. For a cat-sized dinosaur, you'll want about 10 to 15 strips 5 centimetres (2 inches) wide and 40 centimetres (16 inches) long. Depending on the size of the limbs and tail, you'll also want a number of smaller strips. It's better to cut a few more than you think you'll need than to have to stop to cut more when you're up to your elbows in plaster.

Preparing the Plaster

Mix the plaster according to the package directions or use the following method:

1. Pour 250 mL (1 cup) of water into an old plastic or metal bowl or bucket.
2. Take a handful of plaster and sprinkle it into the bowl of water.
3. Watch the plaster disappear.
4. Repeat steps 2 and 3.
5. Continue sprinkling plaster into the water until little islands form on the surface. If the islands disappear, add a bit more plaster. If they don't disappear, wait until they are completely wet, then stick your hand in and mix the plaster around until there are no lumps and the plaster feels thick like cream.

As soon as you've mixed the plaster thoroughly, start dipping burlap strips into it, one at a time. Each strip should be completely soaked in wet plaster. Holding the burlap in one hand, remove excess plaster by pulling the strip between the thumb and forefinger of the other hand. If you're fairly careful, this excess plaster will end up in the bowl and not in your hair or on your shoes.

Wrap the plaster-soaked burlap strips around your sculpture, following the plaster bandage method described on pages 36 and 37. Once you've covered your whole dinosaur, let it set completely. The drying time will vary from an hour to overnight, depending on the type of plaster you use and the temperature of the room. Plaster produces heat while it is setting, so a good rule of thumb is to wait until it becomes cold. Even then, if you can scratch it easily with your fingernail, you should leave it longer. This is good because you're going to need more time to clean up. As I said, this is a lot messier.

If you used a metal bowl to mix your plaster, pour some water into it right away and vigorously clean it with a rag. If you used a flexible plastic bowl, you may wait until the plaster sets, then bang it upside down on a table to knock the plaster out. Keep in mind that this may damage the newly refinished dining room table.

Once it's thoroughly dry, you can turn your sculpture into a one-of-a-kind masterpiece. See pages 43 to 48 for some ideas to get you started.

If you're fairly careful, the excess plaster will end up in the bowl and not in your hair or on your shoes.

Some people use tiny pieces of paper mixed with papier mâché paste to form muscles and noses and things like that. In most cases, I prefer to use dryer lint mixed with the paste to add such details. This becomes a total mess unless you mix it thoroughly and wet your fingers so that it doesn't stick to you.

Papier Mâché

Papier mâché is French for "chewed paper," because it's made with ripped-up pieces of newspaper dipped in paste.

Before you start ripping up all the newspaper, spread some sheets over your work surface. Now you're ready to make the newspaper strips. Hold a single page at the top with both hands. Because of the way the paper fibers lie, newspaper tears much more easily from top to bottom than from side to side. Pull down with one hand and the page will tear all the way to the bottom. You will want different widths, so experiment to see what works.

It's important to always tear your strips. If you use scissors, the strips will have sharp edges that don't blend in well.

There are a frightening number of recipes for making papier mâché paste. Some don't work all that well. Here are two that do work, starting with our favorite.

Papier Mâché Paste
RECIPE #1

1/2 cup (125 mL) all-purpose
 flour or cornstarch
2 cups (500 mL) cold water
2 cups (500 mL) boiling water
 in a pot
3 Tbsp. (75 mL) sugar

Mix the flour and cold water in a bowl. Add the flour mixture to the pot of boiling water and stir it until it returns to a boil. Remove from the heat and stir in the sugar. Wait for it to cool so it doesn't burn your hands.

RECIPE #2

125 mL (1/2 cup) white glue
 or carpenter's glue
125 mL (1/2 cup) water

Pour the glue and water into an old container and stir with a Popsicle stick or spoon. This recipe avoids using the stove and so is safer. But clean-up is harder, especially if you don't do it right away.

(left) Miranda is applying papier mâché strips by herself.

(below) The job goes much faster with a friend's help.

Once you've prepared your paste and newspaper strips, you can begin wrapping your dinosaur. Working with papier mâché is a perfect example of the benefits of helping each other. Working alone, Miranda has to dip newspaper strips into the paste, wipe off the excess, pick up the dinosaur, add the strips, set down the dinosaur, then start again. In the next photograph, Emily and Miranda have decided to work together. Emily dips the strips into the paste and wipes off the excess, then lays the strips down on an ice-cream pail lid. Miranda can simply pick up the strips and wrap them with one hand, while holding her dinosaur with the other. Because she doesn't have to keep setting the dinosaur down to prepare the paper, she can cover her sculpture in much less time.

After two layers of papier mâché have been applied, let them dry completely. The drying time will depend on room temperature and humidity, but should take between 6 and 12 hours. Too many layers of wet papier mâché take forever to dry out. Sometimes they even become moldy and you have to throw your dinosaur in the garbage before it turns into a really scary (and smelly) monster. Prop your dinosaur up while it's drying so that it hardens in the position you want. Make sure its legs are

If you have leftover papier mâché paste, you might want to cover it and save it in the fridge. You can use the paste when you make a home for your dinosaur (see pages 50 to 53).

straight under its body. Use soup cans, shoe boxes—anything that works and is the right height.

A common problem with papier mâché sculptures is that the legs aren't stiff enough. They become floppy, causing the dinosaur to fall over. Sometimes, adding more papier mâché will fix the problem. You can also run stiff wire along the length of the leg and wrap it with tape or papier mâché. However, if you've already painted the legs

or done something else you don't want to cover up, try forcing a piece of stiff wire up through the bottom of the foot, at least 3 centimetres (about an inch) past the weak spot. You will need pliers to do this. Trying to push on the end of a wire with your bare hands is a good way to put a hole in your thumb.

Another great reason to work with your friends is that you can stop now and then to play with your dinosaurs even if they aren't completely finished. Here, two unpainted dinosaurs battle it out, although neither of them has any eyes or teeth!

(left) The wire stand is bent into shape and attached to one leg.

(right) Jordan and Emily painting their dinosaurs.

(below) An assortment of paints and brushes.

Finishing Your Sculpture

You can make your dinosaur look terrific in lots of ways, with paint, eyes, teeth, and seeds or feathers. But first it might need a little help to stand up the way you want. You'll notice that the dinosaur on the left in the photo above has a metal ring attached to one of its feet to keep it from falling over. If you want your dinosaur to have a stand, you might want to make it before you do any painting.

To make the stand, bend a piece of stiff wire as shown above. It should be roughly the shape of a light bulb, with a round loop and two straight ends. Squeeze the straight ends together and tape them with electrician's tape. Now bend the wire so the circle part lies flat on the table and the straight part sticks straight up. When finished, it should look like the halo on a Christmas angel, but upside down. Tape it to the leg of your dinosaur and adjust the ring until your creation stands the way you want.

Painting

Okay, now your dinosaur is standing tall and brave and it's time to color it. Any water-based paint will do, including leftover house paint – or you can pick the exact colors you want at a hobby or art supply store. You'll also want a variety of brushes.

When deciding on colors and patterns for your dinosaur, it's always a good idea to look through picture books about animals for inspiration. Tigers, peacocks, iguanas, leopards, even snakes and fish can give you ideas. We'll never know what colors dinosaurs were, so you can go wild.

(right) When you add the eyes,
dinosaurs really come to life!

(below) Tools and materials
for finishing your sculpture.

(below) Comb teeth make
perfect dinosaur teeth.

Eyes and Teeth

If you really want to go to town,
you can add eyes, teeth, skin
texture and even feathers! The
photograph above displays some
things you might use to dress up
your beast, including rice, grain,
mustard and poppy seeds, cloth
flowers, feathers, and plastic
eyes. All of these are quite easy
to find.

Hobby and craft stores carry
a variety of plastic eyes ranging
from goofy-looking wobbly eyes
to more realistic-looking teddy

bear eyes. If you want to be
downright weird, some even sell
very human-looking doll eyes.
Taxidermy supply stores can be
more expensive, but they sell
many kinds of realistic animal
eyes. Some eyes come on a stem.
To use these, you just poke holes
in your dinosaur's head and push
the eyes in. Other eyes are flat on
the back and can be glued on.

For extra realism, you can
make eyelids. It's a bit tricky
to do, but if you want to try,
first mix dryer lint with either
white glue, or a flour and water
paste, until it's mushy and easy
to shape. Roll out two little
sausages, and place one at the
top of the eye and one at the
bottom. Using a toothpick,

push the top and bottom ends
together at the corners of the eye.

If you want a really dangerous-
looking dinosaur, it's going to
need teeth. In a pinch, you can
use rice or the ends of toothpicks.
But my favorite way to make
teeth in a hurry is to use the teeth
from a comb—preferably a white
comb, unless you want a dinosaur
with blue or red teeth. Snip off
the teeth with wire cutters or
scissors so that they're a little
longer than you want them. Next
you need to poke holes in the
inside of the mouth where you
want the teeth to be.

If you look closely at Emily's dinosaur below, you'll see patches of blue on the head and shoulders. These show where dryer lint paste was used to build up muscles and create brow horns and a bony ridge on the snout. The claws on the dinosaur's toes were made with oat kernels from the bird feeder.

Find something sharp, but not too sharp, to make the holes. You don't want to cut yourself. The end of a pair of tweezers is perfect. If you poke a hole, then drag the tool you are using, it creates a slot instead of just a hole and makes inserting the teeth much easier. Stick the wide end of the tooth into a bit of white glue and then into the hole or slot. This is tricky work. As Emily demonstrates in the photograph at left, it's easier if you use tweezers. When all the teeth are in, use a small brush or a toothpick to fill any gaps with glue. Then let the glue dry before doing any more work on your dinosaur. Otherwise, the teeth will fall out or become crooked.

Now you have a ferocious-looking dinosaur that is ready for action. There is nothing to prevent you from calling it finished, playing with it, making more or whatever you want. There are, however, some things you can do to dress it up even more.

Emily is carefully inserting the teeth.

Skin Texture

Scientists have found a lot of fossils that show us what the skin texture of dinosaurs looked like. Generally, they had beady skin a lot like some of our modern lizards. The size of the beads, called tubercles (**too**-bur-kels) by paleontologists, ranged from tiny to over 5 centimetres (2 inches) across.

Here is an easy way to give your dinosaur neat-looking, pebbly skin using poppy seeds or mustard seeds, which can be bought at any grocery store. Small dinosaurs look good with the small, grayish-black poppy seeds. If you are making a bigger dinosaur, you can use mustard seeds – which are larger – by themselves or mixed with poppy seeds. Brush white glue onto the part of your dinosaur that you want textured, then sprinkle it with seeds. Apply glue to small areas at a time, so it doesn't dry out before you can add the seeds.

Emily's dinosaur will have a pebbly, poppy-seed surface on just the head and legs. Because this is a small dinosaur, she can cover a whole leg with seeds at one time.

You're probably thinking, "What about the rest of the dinosaur?" Well, it's going to get covered with feathers, but not right away. Why? Because, and this is *very important*: Once you

Emily is sprinkling poppy seeds onto a foot that's been glued.

are finished with the seeds, set the dinosaur aside until the glue dries. Give it at least an hour. If you rush, the seeds will get knocked off and stick to things they aren't supposed to, such as the cat or your mom's slippers.

After the glue is dry, you may want to experiment a little. You can create a shiny effect if you paint a mixture of half glue and half water over the seeds. This also makes the seeds stick even better. When it's dry, you can paint over the seeds or leave it as is.

Feathers

If you want your dinosaur to have feathers, you can buy them in different shapes and colors at sport fishing shops and craft supply stores. You can also use the petals of artificial paper or cloth flowers, which are sold at craft stores. Ask if they have any flowers that were damaged in shipping and you may find a bargain. If you are using petals, snip off the petals you want from the flowers.

Organize the different sizes and colors of the petals or feathers in shallow containers. Decide how you'll arrange them on your dinosaur and lay them out on sheets of coarse sandpaper. This keeps them from flying around the room before they're stuck to your dinosaur.

You will attach your petals or feathers starting at the end of the tail and working forward. On the legs, start where the skin texture ends and work forward. The ones coming up the tail and the ones going up the legs meet at the hips. You want them to blend together where they meet in a flowing manner, not butt into each other at right angles. A simple trick that will help you to place them in the right direction is to draw lines on your dinosaur as shown.

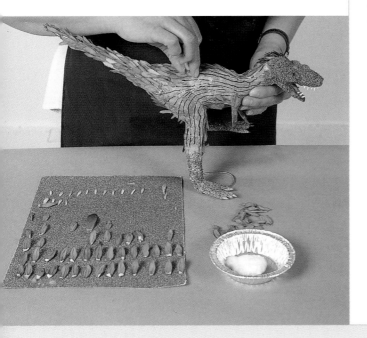

Starting at the tip of the tail and working forward, the feathers are attached following the pattern lines.

Once your feathers or petals are all laid out, paint the tail of your dinosaur with water-based, non-toxic contact cement. You can buy this at most hardware stores. *Do not use regular contact cement.* It is very bad for you and smells awful. In a pinch, you can use ordinary white glue, but there is a tendency for the feathers to slide around or fall off before the glue dries.

Next, dip just the back tip of each petal or feather in the non-toxic contact cement. Lay them in rows on top of two or three sheets of paper. Now take a break for about 15 minutes while the glue dries. Make sure you read the directions on the container for the correct length of time to wait. This is the weird thing about contact cement. It doesn't work if it's wet, but if you apply it to separate surfaces and then press them together after 15 to 30 minutes, they stick together forever. It's like magic! Don't ask me how it works, I have no idea. What I do know is that if you start sticking on feathers too soon or wait too long, it doesn't work.

When you start applying the petals or feathers, make sure the glued ends are always pointing toward the head. You may find that after a while they aren't sticking. Chances are, the contact cement just became too dry to work. If that happens, brush some fresh contact cement onto the dinosaur and wait 5 or 10 minutes, then carry on. The final result is one sporty-looking dinosaur.

Congratulations!

You've created your very own dinosaur. But you probably won't stop at just one. Once you get the hang of it, you may want to check out museum displays and books about dinosaurs to find out all the different kinds you can make. Paleontologists have uncovered hundreds of wonderful dinosaurs and have pieced together some astonishing stories. You and your friends can create herds of horned and duckbilled dinosaurs. Packs of fierce meat-eaters. Giant, long-necked sauropods. There's no limit to the dinosaurs you can make or the stories you can tell.

The world the dinosaurs lived in was quite different from our world today. Generally, it was warmer, and even in northern regions you would have found lots of trees and other plants. Some parts of the world were covered in deserts, just like those of today. We know that many dinosaurs nested in vast colonies and migrated from place to place in herds of thousands! Picture your dinosaurs feeding along a huge river delta that empties into the sea. Or chasing through forests of giant redwoods, palm trees and cycads, which look something like pine cones with a fern growing out of the top.

Environments

Making a home for your dinosaurs can be as much fun as creating the sculptures. You can build a simple landscape using materials around your house. Museum workers call these displays dioramas (die-oh-**ra**-muzz). A scrap of plywood makes a good base. Or use a piece of cardboard, whatever size you like. If you're using cardboard, it's a good idea to tack it to an old board so the corners don't curl up as it dries. Be careful with the tacks if you're making your masterpiece on the dining room table!

It also helps to make a simple sketch before you start your diorama. You may not follow it exactly, but it can be useful to refer to a plan.

If you want to have any water for your dinosaurs, the easiest thing to do is paint on a stream or pond before making the rest of the landscape.

You can make dry land using sand or soil and papier mâché paste. If you want your landscape to have a nesting site or hills, it's easier to make those first, then cover it all at the same time.

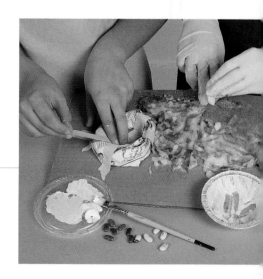

To start your dinosaur nest, tape a circle of rolled-up newspaper to your base. The surrounding landscape is made with dryer lint and papier mâché paste.

To finish the landform, sprinkle sand over
the whole base while the paste is still wet.

The photographs on the next page show a diorama of a nesting site in a desert landscape. We know from fossils that dinosaurs often nested in open areas where there wasn't much plant life. It's easy to create a nest scene using newspaper, masking tape, dryer lint and kidney beans. Roll a sheet of newspaper into a cylinder, then bend it into a circle like a donut. Tape the circle onto the cardboard with masking tape, to make a shape much like the nests of piled-up dirt or sand that some dinosaurs laid their eggs in. Soak dryer lint with papier mâché paste and lay it over and around the newspaper nest.

If you want the nest to be occupied, make some eggs by painting kidney beans white or whatever color you choose. When they're dry, arrange them in the nest.

To make hills or dunes, just tape down wads of newspaper with masking tape, and cover them with dryer lint and papier mâché paste as you would do to make a nest.

Once your terrain is finished, spread papier mâché paste over your base, not too thickly. While

**Materials Needed to Create
a Dinosaur Environment**

- plywood or cardboard
  (for base)
- paints and brushes
- sand or soil
- newspaper
- masking tape
- dryer lint
- kidney or other beans
- papier mâché paste
- backer rod (for trees)
- cloth flowers (for trees)

it's still gooey, sprinkle sand or clean soil over it. Before the paste dries, you can make footprints by pressing one of your dinosaur's feet into the sand or soil. You can also stick small stones into the paste, if you like.

Now your diorama is ready for vegetation. If you have leftover backer rod and cloth flowers from making your dinosaur, you can make cycads or palm trees almost instantly. Cut the backer rod to the size you want. It makes a perfect trunk and even has a little curve that looks quite realistic. Paint it brown. Select some green flower parts or paint petals of other colors green. You can also cut leaves and branches out of construction paper. Pin or tack them to one end of the backer rod. You now have a tree.

Different types of trees can be made using the same wire or newspaper armature methods that were used for making dinosaurs. I'm sure you can invent ways to make other kinds of plants, such as ferns or flowers.

One last thing you might like to make is a painted back-ground to complete your diorama. Cardboard works best for this, because it's easy to cut into a curve if you want. You can paint sky and clouds on the upper part and a landscape on the lower part. It looks great if your painted landscape is similar to your three-dimensional base.

(left) It's great to ask for help, but sometimes the helpers don't know when to quit! Emily's mom, Mary Ann, and her sister, Anna, are adding more sand and finding new ways for the nesting dinosaur to sit on its eggs.

For the scene in the photographs on these pages, the cardboard background was cut in a curve using a sharp knife. Ask someone to help you with the cutting. After it was painted, the background was simply taped to the base.

Your dinosaurs will look right at home in their new environment. But it can get crowded in no time, especially if your friends come over with their beasts. Luckily, it's easy to make more and bigger dioramas. But watch out! You may get lost in time.

You can create any scene imaginable filled with your favorite dinosaurs!

Scientific Names

ALL OF THE ANIMALS
WE ARE FAMILIAR
WITH HAVE NAMES —
SUCH AS LEOPARD,
IGUANA, DUCK
OR EAGLE.

However, these animals are called different names by people speaking different languages, and that creates a great deal of confusion. In order to reduce this confusion every animal, plant and other organism, whether living or extinct, is given a scientific name that is used all over the world. These names are made up primarily of Latin and ancient Greek words.

While an English-speaking person says "duck" and a French-speaking person says "canard," the scientific name in either language is *Anas*, written in italic. *Anas* is the genus name, meaning that it is the first part of the name of all ducks. But what about the different kinds of ducks? There are mallards, pintails, eiders, and many others. These are separate species and they have a second species name that follows the genus. For example, a mallard is *Anas platyrhynchos*.

Dinosaurs are named in the same way, usually by the scientists who discover them or by the scientists who write the first scientific description of them. The word dinosaur itself is Latin for "terrible lizard." Often we refer to dinosaurs by only their genus name, as in Triceratops. Most people are unaware of the many species names, including *Triceratops horridus*, *Triceratops serratus*, *Triceratops flabellatus*, and more. Sometimes the species name honors the person who found it or refers to where it was found, and sometimes it describes an outstanding feature of the dinosaur.

Here is a list of the dinosaurs mentioned in this book with their full scientific names and meanings.

Albertosaurus libratus
powerful Alberta lizard

Archaeopteryx lithographica
ancient wing from lithographic stone

Confuciusornis sanctus
sacred Confucius bird

Dromaeosaurus albertensis
emu lizard from Alberta

Iguanodon mantelli
iguana tooth (found by Dr. Gideon) Mantell

Protarchaeopteryx robusta
robust with primitive ancient wing

Protoceratops andrewsi
primitive horn face (found by Roy Chapman) Andrews

Sinornithosaurus millenii
Chinese bird-reptile of the millenium

Tyrannosaurus rex
tyrant lizard king

Velociraptor mongoliensis
swift stealer from Mongolia

Index

About the Authors

BRIAN COOLEY GREW UP IN PINCHER CREEK, ALBERTA. As a child he drew, painted and sculpted constantly. He collected toy dinosaurs and read science fiction as well as dinosaur stories.

When he finished high school he enrolled in the Alberta College of Art, where he majored in sculpting. In his late twenties he had his first opportunity to sculpt dinosaurs professionally. Since then he has become an internationally acclaimed dinosaur sculptor. He has produced models for such prestigious magazines as *National Geographic* and for permanent display around the world – for The Field Museum of Natural History in Chicago, Disney World in Orlando, The Academy of Natural Sciences in Philadelphia, the world-famous Royal Tyrrell Museum of Palaeontology in Drumheller, Alberta, Canada, and the Fukui Dinosaur Museum in Japan.

Mary Ann Wilson was born in Whitehorse, Yukon and spent her teen years in southern Alberta. She, too, attended the Alberta College of Art, where she majored in painting. She has worked alongside Brian in bringing dinosaurs to life since he began sculpting professionally.

Brian and Mary Ann currently live in Calgary, Alberta with their two daughters.